# Working Together Against

# VIOLENCE AGAINST WOMEN

Increasing awareness is an important step in stopping violence against women.
The message on the above billboard attempts to encourage the public to get
involved in the fight against domestic violence.

❖ THE LIBRARY OF SOCIAL ACTIVISM ❖

Working Together Against

# VIOLENCE AGAINST WOMEN

## Aliza Sherman

THE ROSEN PUBLISHING GROUP, INC.
NEW YORK

*Special Thanks*
*The author would like to thank the women interviewed in this book. Special thanks to Stacey Kabat from Peace at Home for allowing us to reprint excerpts from her handbook. Thanks to Ruel Espejo and Kay Johnson for additional research. Also, thanks to KK for endless support.*

Published in 1996 by The Rosen Publishing Group, Inc.
29 East 21st Street, New York, NY 10010

First Edition

**Library of Congress Cataloging-in-Publication Data**

Sherman, Aliza.
    Working together against violence against women / Aliza Sherman.
       p.   cm. — (The library of social activism)
    Includes bibliographical references and index.
    Summary: Explores the issue of violence against women and discusses the ways to become involved locally and nationally to stop its occurrence.
    ISBN 0-8239-2258-8
    1. Women—Crimes against—Juvenile literature. 2. Violent crimes—Prevention—Juvenile literature. 3. Abused women—Juvenile literature [1. Women—Crimes against. 2. Abused women. 3. Violence. 4. Violent crimes.] I. Title. II. Series.
HV6250.4.W65S533  1996
362.82'927—dc20                               96-9909
                                                 CIP
                                               AC

*Manufactured in the United States of America*

# Contents

# INTRODUCTION

**HI! I'M CAROL POTTER. YOU MAY**
remember me from the television show *Beverly Hills, 90210*. I played Cindy Walsh, Brenda and Brandon's mom. What you may not know about me is that for more than ten years I have been working against domestic violence.

Why did I choose to get involved in this issue? Because being unsafe in your own home and afraid of someone you love is frightening. Home is where we're all supposed to be safe. And I realized that violence doesn't just happen to other people. It can happen to anyone, to a friend or relative. It can even happen to me.

Why should you know about violence against women? Because anyone can be a victim of domestic violence. You don't have to be married, or even living together with someone. Women need to be provided with information so they can make themselves safer, recognize situations that could become dangerous, and reach out to other women who have been hurt.

Men can be affected by violence as well. It can happen to their loved ones. They need to understand the root of violence and see how their own feelings and attitudes might make others think domestic violence is okay. They also need to let other men know that it's wrong.

But what can you do to help end this problem? The only way that violence against women will end is if society says it must. Society consists of institutions and organizations that can help. But mostly it consists of people like you and me working together to make the world a safer place.

This book provides a lot of information about violence against women. You'll find answers to your questions and read stories about women who have made a difference. You'll also find places where you can get help or offer your help to end this terrible problem. The life you save could be your mother's, your sister's, your wife's, your friend's, or even your own.

### ❖ QUESTIONS TO ASK YOURSELF ❖

The problem of violence against women is so widespread that even television stars like Carol Potter are working against it. 1) Do you think that wide publicity will be helpful? 2) How could other stars help in the fight? 3) How could you help?

The violence in an abusive relationship is likely to become worse as time passes. It's important to recognize the warning signs and seek help before it's too late.

# chapter

# 1

# WHAT IS VIOLENCE AGAINST WOMEN?

YOU HAVE ONLY TO READ THE NEWSPAPER OR watch the news on television to know that violence against women is a growing problem in our neighborhoods and cities. You may have heard about a little girl named Megan in New Jersey who was raped and murdered by her next-door neighbor, a convicted sex offender. Or it might be a young girl named Polly in California who was kidnapped during a slumber party and found dead a few weeks later. Or it might be a woman who was beaten, raped, and left for dead in Central Park in New York City late one night. Or it might be a woman in Brooklyn, New York, who was stalked by a man she used to date and shot in the head because she wouldn't go out with him anymore.

These are just a few examples of the violence against women that occur in the United States every day. These brutal crimes and their victims have touched many people and inspired them to take action against violence against women.

The trial of O. J. Simpson for the murders of his former wife, Nicole Brown Simpson, and her friend, Ronald Goldman, heightened public awareness of the problem of domestic violence.

### ❖ DOMESTIC VIOLENCE ❖

Domestic violence is physical abuse that happens within a family. Anyone can be a victim of domestic violence: women, children, and men. However, in most cases the men are the abusers, and the women are the victims.

There was one case, however, that the country watched for months and brought much attention to domestic violence. The murder trial of former sports superstar O. J. Simpson for the brutal murders of his former wife, Nicole Brown Simpson, and her friend, Ronald Goldman, captured the country's attention. As evidence, the prosecution used Simpson's history of physical violence toward his former wife, including pictures of her bruises from being beaten and her 911 call for help. Simpson was eventually acquitted (found innocent) of the crime of murder, but the trial raised public awareness of the problem of domestic violence.

### ❖ MOLLY ❖

*Molly was fourteen years old when she started dating Ben, the neighborhood rebel. "All the girls thought he was charming and great in a sort of bad-boy way," explained Molly. They started dating and things got more and more serious throughout the rest of her high school years. But when Molly was ready to go to college, Ben couldn't let go. "I think he felt like he was being left behind. So he started visiting me at my college," Molly said. "The violence happened gradually."*

*Ben had been collecting weapons, such as swords and knives. He began to threaten Molly with them. "I basically thought it was my fault. I had a temper that would flare up. When he got mad at me for it, I automatically assumed that I was to blame." For three years, the violence continued and got worse. Soon, Molly was bruised all the time. Ben was barred from her school twice.*

*When Molly couldn't take the violence anymore, she looked for a support group in the Yellow Pages. In her first meeting with the group, she met a woman who had lost everything because of a violent marriage—her house, her money, her job. The woman*

*lived in a tiny apartment, was going back to school,
and she was happy because she was free from violence. Molly admired this woman and thought, "If
she can do it, I can do it too."*

*It took a few years before Molly was finally free
and felt safe from Ben. Although he continued to
stalk her, her friends and family devised special
plans to protect her, such as answering or screening
her phone calls.*

One of the results of domestic abuse is that
women who have been abused for a long period
of time begin to believe they are at fault. Like
Molly, they believe *their* behavior or attitude
causes their husbands or boyfriends to hit them.
Many women begin to think of the abuse as a
normal part of life. They believe being beaten,
hit or slapped, or forced to have sex is normal.
But violence is *not* normal. No one has the right
to touch a girl's or a woman's body against her
will, even if that person is her husband,
boyfriend, or father.

Studies have shown that Americans are more
likely to be seriously injured or killed by a family
member than they are by a stranger. According
to the Family Violence Protection Fund, in 1994
almost 4 million American women were physically abused by their husbands or boyfriends.
The actual number may be even higher than statistics indicate, because many women are afraid

to report the abuse. It is estimated that every nine seconds, a woman is abused in the United States. According to the Uniform Crime Report of the Federal Bureau of Investigation (FBI), 30 percent of the total number of women killed in 1990 in the United States died at the hands of a husband or boyfriend. More than 800 women were killed by their husbands, and more than 400 were killed by their boyfriends.

## ❖ RAPE—A VIOLENT ACT ❖

According to the FBI, a woman is raped every three minutes. However, this figure does not account for the many cases that go unreported. Many victims of rape have a hard time dealing with their feelings of frustration, anger, guilt, and shame. These feelings can keep them from reporting the crime to the police or even telling a friend, or relative.

The legal definition of rape varies from state to state. In many states it includes the lack of consent, force or threat of force, and sexual penetration. There are also different types of rape, including:

- Random rape, or rape by a stranger.
- Incest, or rape by a family member or relative. Most victims of this type of rape are young children. However, this kind of sexual abuse within a family can go on for

years, especially as a young woman begins
to mature and develop during puberty.

- Child molestation, or sexual molestation of
children. This is when someone outside the
family, usually an adult, forces a child to
have sexual intercourse or be part of other
sexual acts. There have been cases where
children were sexually abused by teachers,
religious clergy, or family acquaintances.
- Date rape, or rape by someone the victim
knows, such as a friend or boyfriend. This
type of rape often goes unreported because
many victims don't want to see their
boyfriends go to jail. Sometimes they may
not even believe they've been raped. This is
especially true if they are involved in an
abusive relationship and are confused
because of continuing violence and abuse.
- Marital rape happens between a married
couple. Marital rape is illegal in every state,
but each state defines this crime differently.
Many women are afraid to report this kind
of rape because, like date rape victims, they
don't want to send their husbands to jail.
Or they may not think people will believe
them. In many cases, the woman may not
even believe that it was rape because the
man was her husband.

Rape is the most violent act that a male can

carry out on a female. When a male rapes a
female, he is often not really interested in sex.
Sometimes, a rapist is acting out his anger at a
female in his life who may have abused him or
who he feels has hurt him in some way.

### ❖ PORNOGRAPHY—DOES IT ❖ ENCOURAGE VIOLENCE AGAINST WOMEN?

The issue of pornography is one that has
existed for a long time. Many well-known feminist writers, such as Andrea Dworkin and
Catherine MacKinnon, define pornography as
the vivid portrayal of women performing sexual
acts. Pornographers claim to be providing
people, usually males, with magazines, books,
films, and videos to fulfill the sexual fantasies of
their audience. Some of these materials include
violence against women as a part of sexual plea-
sure. People who oppose pornography say that
women are treated as tools for fulfilling men's
sexual desires. They say that women are often
treated as "things" or "objects" instead of
people. Opposers also say that some men may
get used to thinking of women as objects and
not as human beings. Because of this, some men
may think it is okay to treat a woman without
respect or with violence or sexual aggression.

Many states have laws against showing pornographic material in places that are open for all to
see. But there are places where it is still shown

in public areas. For example, most video stores have an "adult" section for pornography that is separated from the rest of their video products. But there are still video stores that continue to show pornographic titles in the same area as mainstream videos. This means that children and teenagers may see pornographic material even while browsing for a favorite cartoon or the latest action movie. When they unexpectedly see these pornographic images, they may think that it is okay to treat women as sexual objects or in degrading ways.

## ❖ VIOLENCE ABROAD ❖

Violence against women does not exist only in the United States; it exists everywhere. The following are examples of the violence happening against women in countries around the world today.

- In South Africa, battered women reported police officers who, when called to investigate domestic abuse, would instead sit and share drinks with the abusing husbands.
- In 1994, many women in Canada were outraged by a judge's decision that a man accused of abusing and raping his wife could use drunkenness as a valid defense.
- In 1994, Islamic believers in Algeria shot and killed three young women on their way

The 1995 United Nations Fourth World Conference on Women in Beijing, China, provided a forum to address many of the problems that women face around the world. Above, a Bangladeshi delegate conducts a silent protest against the practice of population control.

to school for not observing the *hijab* (the wearing of a large head scarf), which is required of women and girls.

- In 1994, hundreds of Somali women were raped in refugee camps in Somalia, according to a report by the Women's Rights Project and Africa Watch (Human Rights Watch).
- In India, some women are killed because their dowry (the wealth a wife is required to bring to her husband's family as part of the marriage contract) is thought to be too small by the husband's family. In a "dowry death," a woman is sprayed with gasoline, lit on fire, and burned alive. The Indian government has proposed a bill to protect women from such attacks by making them punishable by death.

Although the statistics are bleak, there is good news. Many countries are beginning to take action against violence against women.

- In 1994, for the first time, authorities in Chile classified domestic violence as a crime.
- In 1995, a "Zero Tolerance" campaign was launched in Scotland against domestic violence. Posters protesting the violence were seen in England and Ireland as well.

- In 1995, Canada banned firearms not used for hunting or sports purposes. The government also enforced stricter sentences for improper use of firearms and required the registration of all firearms to help combat domestic violence.

Another event that brought international attention to the problem of violence against women was the United Nations Fourth World Conference on Women, in Beijing, People's Republic of China. The conference focused on violence, health, education, and other important issues concerning the welfare of women throughout the world. The conference increased world awareness of the problems faced by women in many countries and examined possible solutions to them.

### ❖ VIOLENCE—IT AFFECTS US ALL ❖

Violence against women is a tremendous problem that exists all around the world. This violence affects all of us. There are women who face dangers in their homes and on the streets. They face the danger of being beaten, raped, or killed every day. These women can be found as far away as a different country or as close as your neighborhood, building, or even in your own home. These women live in a constant state of fear. But there are ways to help these women.

Many people are working together to make the world safer for women. You can become a part of this effort.

### ❖ QUESTIONS TO ASK YOURSELF ❖

Violence against women has ruined many lives and torn apart many families. 1) What are some forms of violence that women face? 2) Are there organizations or women's shelters in your town or community that help women who have been abused or raped?

# chapter

# 2

# WHY IS THERE VIOLENCE AGAINST WOMEN?

THERE ARE MANY CAUSES FOR THE VIOLENCE that occurs against women. Some people wrongly put the blame on women. Girls at an early age are told to behave and dress appropriately so as not to attract unwanted attention. You may remember being told not to flirt or talk to strangers, and not to go out late by yourself. Meanwhile, the rowdy or violent behavior of some boys is excused because, "Boys will be boys." This gives many people the wrong message that girls and women are responsible for unwanted and sometimes threatening male attention. But putting the blame on women excuses men from taking responsibility for their own behavior. We need to examine the real causes of violence and find possible solutions.

## ❖ THE HISTORY OF PREJUDICE ❖ AGAINST WOMEN

The United States has a history of sexism,

or bias against women. This means that many people in society, especially men, have looked down on women and held them back in many ways. The United States was founded by white men who owned property and had the right to vote in this new country. Their homes, their wives, and their children were considered to be their property. A law in the United States permitted a man to beat his wife as long as the stick he used was not thicker than his thumb. This is where the phrase "rule of thumb" comes from. Many men thought that women were weaker and could not handle school or work. Because women were expected to stay home to keep the house in order and raise the children, they were prevented from being part of public life or from receiving an education.

Women did not win the right to vote until the early 1900s. Even after they won the right to vote, men's biased attitudes towards women were slow to change. It took many more years of struggle before women were able to hold public office or get jobs traditionally held by men or be promoted to managerial positions or other positions of power.

## ❖ UPBRINGING AND FAMILY ❖
### BACKGROUND

Young people are easily influenced by things they see around them, but the most important

Some women remain in violent relationships because they are embarrassed or afraid to share their problem with people who can help.

influences in their lives are their mothers and fathers. With many families breaking up, children may live in homes with only one parent. Because of this, many children may not be able to see positive relationships between two adults. With drug use becoming an increasing problem in many homes, many children grow up in homes where one or both parents are addicted to drugs or alcohol. And when children see their fathers beating their mothers, they form ideas about how men and women treat each other. They may assume that it is normal for a man to disrespect or abuse a woman.

If there are no positive role models in the home, where do young people find support or someone to look up to? How do they learn what is right or wrong? There are other adults that teens can turn to who can be stable and positive role models. These role models can show positive ways of behaving and give hope to desperate teens. These adults could be relatives, teachers, clergy members, or neighbors.

## ❖ MEDIA INFLUENCES ❖

Another factor that has a strong influence in the lives of teens is the media. Many teens turn to television and movies for entertainment. However, TV shows and movies often contain disturbing scenes of sex and violence in which people are maimed or killed and women are attacked or raped. This increase in the level of violence in the media has led many people to question how the violence and other negative images affect children and teens. Teens are exposed to these images every time they turn on their television set or go to see a movie.

It isn't hard to realize that even before television and movies, there was violence in the world, including violence against women. Do movies and TV shows help change people's attitudes, or do people's attitudes change because of other conditions and then movies and TV shows are made that express the new attitudes? That is a hard question to answer. Fifty years ago, movies had very little sexual content or violence,

Children and teenagers are strongly influenced by what they see on television or in movies. The increase in the level of violence in the media has led to widespread concern about how youth are affected by negative images.

especially the most popular movies of the day. Today, many movies seem to show more sex and violence than ever before.

If a child watches a movie with a parent and has the chance to talk about the violence in the movie, the child may be less likely to imitate the movie or think the violence is okay. If a child watches the same movie and the violence is similar to what he or she sees in the neighborhood every day, the child may end up acting out the parts on the big screen. If a boy sees a music video where a rapper calls a girl by a negative name, he might think it is cool and begin to do the same thing. If a girl sees the same video, she may assume it is normal for men to treat women with disrespect. Her self-confidence may sink.

### ❖ FINDING SOLUTIONS ❖

We've come a long way in getting more rights for women in society, in the workplace, and in the home. We still have a long way to go to create a safer place, not only for women and girls, but for everyone. To make this happen, we all need to join forces and work together. You can make a difference.

### ❖ QUESTIONS TO ASK YOURSELF ❖

Violence against women is not a new problem. It existed when the United States was first established. 1) What rights did women have in

the colonies? 2) Who are the most important influences on a child? 3) How do TV shows and movies affect the way a child or teenager views violent behavior?

# chapter

# 3

# PEOPLE WHO ARE MAKING A DIFFERENCE

MANY PEOPLE, MEN AND WOMEN, ARE trying to change negative attitudes about women and help stop violence against women. Their stories have influenced others to do the same.

## ❖ PEACE AT HOME ❖

Stacey Kabat is a human rights activist. She used to work with refugees and with people around the world who had survived government torture. Now she works in an organization called Peace at Home in Boston. It is a human rights agency that addresses domestic violence through education and prevention programs. In 1994, Stacey won an Academy Award for coproducing the short documentary film "Defending Our Lives" about women who are in prison for killing, in self-defense, the men who beat them.

Stacey is the daughter and granddaughter of battered women. In graduate school she began to work in a battered women's shelter in Boston.

There she met women and children who shared her "family secret." She listened to their stories about violence in their homes and suddenly realized that she, her brother, and her mother were not alone in their experiences. Then she saw an episode of *The Phil Donahue Show* about battered women on television. "I remember calling my mom and the two of us sitting there on the phone together and going, 'Oh, my God. Listen to her. She's telling our story. That happened to us. Maybe it wasn't our fault. It happened to her and she looks okay. She doesn't look bad or crazy or weird.' "

Two years later, Stacey started working with women in a Massachusetts prison as a domestic violence/substance abuse counselor. There she met a group of women who had defended their lives against their batterers. "Through hearing their stories, I realized that I had to start using the tools that I had learned in human rights and [apply] them to domestic violence," Stacey explained. Stacey compares stories of refugees and torture survivors to those of battered women. Some of these stories are of women being emotionally or verbally abused or raped. Also stories of women being beaten until their eyes are blackened or their bones are broken.

Stacey began to document the stories of these women. She also started keeping track of the number of women murdered in Boston. She

began writing down their names, the date they were killed, where they were from, how they were killed, and who killed them. She published the lists. She sent copies to the Governor's Office, to the newspapers, and to the legislature to draw attention to the women who were killed and to the problem of violence against women. Within seven months, the state of Massachusetts declared a public emergency. Stacey has been working with her city and state government ever since to protect women and children from violence in the home.

"Looking back at the development of our society here in the United States, women were very much considered property; and who had the right to vote? Only white, property-owning men, not women, people of color, or children. I think it's important for people to see a historical perspective and to realize how far we've come and yet how much farther we can go. Change is possible, and because of the democratic process, we can be involved to change things. The movement to stop violence against women hasn't just started; it's pretty old. I think the reason the violence happens is [because of] the belief that a male partner has the right to treat the members of his family as property."

Stacey believes that it is important for teens to set up a peer network to share information with other people and assist others in getting

You and your friends can work together to send the message out that violence against women is not condoned by your school, peers, or community.

information about violence. These young people can set up awareness programs or seminars and invite speakers to educate others. They can have information drives in the schools and in community centers. They should talk about how it is not cool to hurt someone else. "So, for some reason, we live in a time when people have forgotten the bottom line that all people deserve a standard of human rights—period. Young people have got to start talking that up."

Stacey says that peer networks should also demand that their school faculty and their community leaders support them and work together not only to fight the violence problems but to make others aware of the problems. According to Stacey, many people don't know about the problems or recognize warning signs of violence. Those who know about the problems don't necessarily know what to do about them or how to help. Information, making others aware of the crisis and the options available, will help fight the problems.

### ❖ MY SISTER'S PLACE ❖

Melinda Kaiser is the educational coordinator of My Sister's Place, a nonprofit agency that provides services to battered women and their children. Melinda is a former battered woman. She got out of her abusive relationship, went back to school for her Master's degree, and did an internship at My Sister's Place. That's how she began working to stop violence against women and children.

Melinda is now in charge of a school-based program that started in 1981. She works directly with junior and senior high school students, usually within their health classes. She and her coworkers go to the classes for a couple of days and talk to the students about the roots of abuse. They discuss the methods used by the abuser, the early warning signs, and the resources available for victims of abuse.

"Students come to us who are being abused at home; someone they know, a family member

Try to be supportive and sensitive to the needs of a friend or family member who has been a victim of violence. Encourage her to contact professional help for information and guidance.

or friend is being abused; or, they're in an abusive relationship themselves. Or this is something they grew up with. . . . We're basically saying, it's okay to talk about it. For some of these kids, it's the first time they've been given permission to do that." Melinda also holds group discussions for the teens. They have co-ed groups (boys and girls) where they have general relationship discussions. Abuse is just one issue. Other groups are designed specifically for young women who have been abused in past relationships. These groups also teach women about the warning signs of violent behavior in a relationship.

"A lot of kids come from single-parent families. There isn't a mother or a father in the home. Some of these kids are teen parents themselves. The models for relationships just aren't there. In other instances, they come from intact, relatively normal, healthy families, and they still don't know. It is one thing to have a role model but another thing actually to be in a situation yourself. For instance, I didn't come from an abusive family, but one of the things I always noticed was that when my parents had a disagreement they never argued in front of the kids. It looked to me as if my parents never argued. So I never saw how things were resolved. The message I got was, if you are in a good relationship, there is no arguing.

"Abuse is a pattern of behavior that one person uses to gain power and control over another person. In an abusive situation, one person feels that he or she has the right to dominate the situation and the relationship. These people often feel that their rights are more important than their partner's rights. They will use methods, tactics as we call them, to gain this control," Melinda explains. "We define physical abuse and sexual abuse, and we talk of weapons, incest, rape, harassment. We talk about tactics such as coercion, threats, the isolation that occurs, and extreme jealousy."

Melinda believes that society is harder on the

person who is being abused than on the abuser. "We always ask 'why is she staying?', and never ask 'Why is he doing this?' We don't speak up as a society, and say 'You can't do this. I don't want to hang around you if you're doing this'.

"Teens are in a really good position to change things because of peer pressure. Peer influence is [very] important . . . in a teen's life. If you see something, call the police. Say something, not just something supportive to the person being abused, but confront the abuser. Don't laugh at jokes about violence against women. Students can work to put together a school program for the entire school. Put posters up, have speakers, and organize workshops. Put signs up that mark this as a violence-free zone. You put this stuff together and you send the message loud and clear that this is something that will not be accepted by the school, by your peers, or by your community."

### ❖ QUESTIONS TO ASK YOURSELF ❖
People can make a difference, even one by one. 1) What did Stacey do to help women in prison? 2) Where did Melinda work for battered women? 3) Could you start a program in your school?

# chapter

# 4

# WHAT YOU CAN DO IN YOUR COMMUNITY

YOU MAY NOT THINK THAT YOU, AS ONE person, can make a difference in the effort to stop violence against women. But you should realize that you can be a very important part of any effort to stop things that are bad and to change things for the better. You don't have to donate a lot of money to organizations that help women, such as battered women's shelters and rape crisis centers, in order to make a difference. You can be a great help by simply stopping at a shelter to donate some clothes or food, or to volunteer your services. Your time is very valuable. Take a moment to write a letter to your state representative, to join a protest against violence against women, or to teach others about the problem. These are some powerful and important ways to make a difference.

- Volunteer to work at local battered women's shelters, rape crisis centers, or hot lines.

You can take a self-defense course or organize one with your friends at school to learn how to avoid dangerous situations and protect yourself from violent attacks.

Many of these places and organizations have very little money or support to help women and children who are victims of violence. Many of them will train you to be an assistant at their center or to answer their hot lines.

- Organize a group with your friends or fellow students to learn more about the problem of violence against women. Help make your neighbors, your fellow students at school, and the people in your community aware. Then you can talk about ways that each of you can help stop violence against women in your area. Making people aware of the problem is the first step. Next you need to discuss ways to solve the problem.

- Learn how to protect yourself physically. Take a self-defense course or organize one at your school with your friends. Learning how to defend yourself can help you avoid dangerous situations, confront an abusive person, and survive violent attacks. It can also increase your self-confidence.

- Organize an event at your school, such as a musical concert, and design posters with a message to draw attention to the problem of violence against women. The money you raise from this event can then be donated to a local group that helps women.

### ❖ QUESTIONS TO ASK YOURSELF ❖

Community activism can go a long way in protecting women and children. 1) What are some possible things you could do to help out at a battered women's shelter? 2) Could you talk to school administrators about organizing a self-defense course for your fellow students?

## chapter

# 5

# WHAT YOU CAN DO IN YOUR STATE AND COUNTRY

❖ **LINA** ❖

*We learned about the problem of violence against women in one of my classes. I was totally shocked. I had no idea that the problem was so bad. There could be women who are being abused right in my neighborhood, and I would never know about it. The more I thought about it, the angrier I got. No one should be afraid to walk down a street or be afraid in her own home. I really want to do something to help stop the violence that many women face every day. But I'm just one person. What can I possibly do that would make a difference?*

Many people feel the same way as Lina. They think they can't make a difference and so choose to do nothing. But there are many ways you can make your voice heard. With a simple phone call or letter to your state representative about a problem you're concerned about, you can make a big difference. When a government

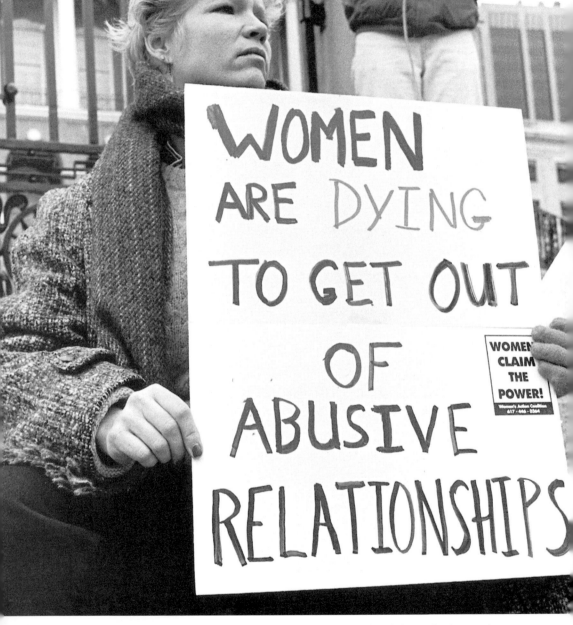

You can make a difference in the fight against domestic violence by becoming active in your state and country. One way to show your support for women's rights is to participate in an antiviolence rally.

official receives one letter or one phone call, he or she knows there are other people who share the same opinion but didn't make the effort to voice it. In this same way, you can also change what you see on television or in the movies. If a commercial or advertisement shows women in a negative way or a TV program shows violence against women, your letter or phone call can make a difference in preventing such shows or ads from airing.

When writing a letter, whether it's to government officials or TV stations, keep the following in mind:

1. State the issue you want to discuss in a brief, but clear manner.
2. State your feelings on the matter and support them with strong reasons or statistics. You can get many statistics from books, newspapers, magazines, or pamphlets, which you should be able to find in your school or local library.
3. Explain why you want the person's support and why that person should support your request. If the letter is to a representative, he or she will often listen to you because you or your parents are voters. If the letter is addressed to a company or TV program, it too is likely to respond to public opinion because it relies on the

## SAMPLE LETTER

Here is a sample letter to a government representative about a specific issue. You can use it as a model for a letter you may want to write on an issue that you are concerned about.

Your Name
Your street address
City, State Zip Code

Name of person to whom you are writing
Title of person
Name of organization or company
Street address, floor or suite number
City, State Zip Code

Dear (Name):

We, the undersigned, want to protest Judge Smith's decision to free John Doe after he was arrested for breaking into his wife's home and beating her. His wife, Helen, suffered many bruises on her body and her arm was broken as a result of John's attack. Judge Smith excused John's vicious act by saying it was an act of passion because Helen left him. Domestic violence is not an act of passion. It is a crime. There is no difference between a man attacking another man on the street and a man attacking his wife in their home.

We, the undersigned, ask that you take a closer look into Judge Smith's ability to be a fair and impartial judge. We hope that you will lend your voice to supporting the cause of protecting women against domestic violence.

Sincerely,

Many Signatures

public to buy its products or watch its programs.

### ❖ OTHER WAYS TO HELP ❖

The problem of violence against women may seem too big for one person to solve, but it is important to remember that many other people are working on making positive changes in your state and country. They may be working in different ways or different organizations, but they are all working together toward the goal of ending the violence problem. By adding your voice and time to any of the following activities, you can really help.

- You can participate in rallies, marches, protests, and events to show your support for women's rights. To find out more about these activities, contact women's organizations in your area such as a chapter of NOW (National Organization for Women), your state coalition against domestic violence, or your local battered women's shelter or rape crisis center. They usually know of events and sometimes organize their own.
- You can join national groups for young activists such as Third Wave. Check with local chapters of NOW or Feminist Majority in Washington, DC, for information on groups for young people to help stop

Above, women gather in front of the Boston state house in 1993 to demonstrate against violence against women.

violence against women and improve the treatment of women in our society.

- Get active in local or national politics. You may be too young to run for office or even too young to vote right now, but you can write letters, sign petitions, and write articles for your school or local paper. You can also speak out to help change and improve laws to better protect women.
- You can even help groups that work on international human rights issues such as Amnesty International and Women's Rights Project, a division of the Human Rights Watch. These groups may have local chapters, but the work they do affects people

throughout the world. We have already learned that violence against women is an international problem. By working with human rights organizations, you can help bring an end to violence against women around the world.

Despite the progress made to stop violence against women, there are still a lot more changes to be made. You can make a difference in bringing forth these changes. You can also work together with your friends, school officials, local community, or national or international organizations to help improve the way women and girls are treated. Sometimes, making a difference is as simple as picking up the phone or writing a letter.

### ❖ QUESTIONS TO ASK YOURSELF ❖

Many people are not even aware of the violence in their neighborhoods. Letters to government officials can be a very effective way of increasing public awareness. 1) Can you get in touch with NOW or other organizations and join them in an organized protest? 2) Are you old enough to vote? Are you familiar with the politics in your community? Why not prepare for your first vote by learning all you can about politics in your town and state.

If you want to help a friend who is involved in an abusive relationship, you can contact local support groups for information on how to help.

# chapter

# 6

# WHAT YOU CAN DO TO HELP A FRIEND

**IF YOU ARE BEING ABUSED, INFORMATION IS** available from several organizations that can help (see the special phone numbers in the back of this book). Get help as soon as you can. Violence in a relationship is likely to become worse. You should know that you deserve to be safe. You must find the strength to get out of a dangerous relationship.

If you know someone—a friend or relative who is being abused—you can help that person in several ways. You may want your friend to leave her abuser, but remember that your friend must want to leave. Don't force her to do any-thing against her wishes. When your friend needs someone to talk to, let her know that you're available. It's important to make her feel as comfortable as possible because she may feel embarrassed about the abuse. Your friend may be confused. She may not realize that the abuse is not normal. She may even feel guilty because she feels somehow responsible for the abuse.

Share your opinions about the abuse in a sensitive and nonjudgmental way. Be supportive rather than critical. Instead of saying something like "I can't believe you put up with him. You're so stupid," you might say, "No one deserves to be treated that way. Don't blame yourself, because it's not your fault." The fact that your friend is willing to talk to you about the problem means she is looking for help and a way out.

Before you offer your friend any advice, contact professional help for vital information and guidance. Look in the Yellow Pages under "Social & Human Services" for organizations that help women who are victims of abuse. Do some research at your local library to find out the laws concerning domestic violence in your state and how the law can protect someone from an abuser. See if there is a women's support group in your area where other victims of domestic abuse share their feelings and important information about what can be done about the problem. Once you have this information and know the options available, you should share them with your friend.

It's important that your friend understand that domestic violence is neither normal nor acceptable. Make it clear to her that the abuse is not her fault. Help her recognize the early warning signs of abuse. And let her know that violence in a relationship will only get worse. She should know that she needs to leave an abusive relationship before it's too late. Once your friend is aware of possible solutions to her problem, she may be more willing to get help. But no matter how much you care about your friend's safety, you should always remember to be respectful of her feelings and wishes. Don't try to force her to do anything she is not ready for.

When she makes the decision to leave the abusive relationship, she will need your support. Try to be there when she needs someone to talk to. And stress the importance of following certain safety plans so that she is protected from danger in the future. For example, you could devise a plan with her to always have a friend or relative available to drive her home if she stays out late at night. Or come up with a secret code that she can use if she is in danger and needs help. When she gives the code, contact the police. You or someone else can also call her at work or home a few times a day to check that she is okay. The next page provides more important information about the steps you can take to help your friend or loved one.

### ❖ STEPS TO HELP A FRIEND ❖

Do you know someone in an abusive relationship? Do you suspect that a friend, relative, or someone you know is being abused? If so, don't be afraid to offer help—you just might save someone's life. Here are some basic steps you can take to assist someone who may be a target of domestic violence.

**Approach** her in an understanding, nonblaming way. Tell her that she is not alone, that there are many women like her in the same kind of situation. Tell her it takes strength to survive and enough trust in someone to talk about battering.

**Acknowledge** that is it scary and difficult to talk about domestic violence. Tell her she doesn't deserve to be threatened, hit, or beaten. Nothing she can do or say makes the abuser's violence OK.

**Share information.** Discuss the roots of violence and how abuse is based on power and control.

**Support her as a friend.** Be a good listener. Encourage her to express her feelings of hurt and anger. Allow her to make her own decisions, even if it means she isn't ready to leave the abusive relationship.

**Ask if she has suffered physical harm.** Go with her to the hospital to check for injuries. Help her report the assault to the police, if she chooses to do so.

**Provide information on help** available to battered women and their children, including social services, emergency shelters, counseling services, and legal advice. To find this information, start with the Yellow Pages.

**Inform her about legal protection** that is available in most states under abuse prevention laws. Go with her to district, probate, or superior court to get a restraining order to prevent further harassment by the abuser. If you can't go, find someone who can.

**Plan safe strategies for leaving an abusive relationship.** These are often called "safety plans." Never encourage someone to follow a safety plan that she believes will put her at further risk.

*Printed with special permission from Peace at Home (Boston)*

❖ QUESTIONS TO ASK YOURSELF ❖
You may have a friend who is in a difficult

situation. You can help, but you need to be sure of some things. 1) Is she ready to leave? 2) Can you provide sources of help for her to contact? 3) Did you help her create "safety" plans for leaving the abusive relationship?

# chapter

# 7

# WE CAN WORK TOGETHER

IF YOU WANT TO MAKE A DIFFERENCE IN THE world, you need to make changes. First, you need to look closely at yourself, then at the people around you. If you are a guy, what are your attitudes toward women and girls? Why do you feel the way you do? How do your friends talk about or treat women and girls? Something as simple as asking your friends to stop calling girls names or making bad jokes about them can be a way of changing attitudes.

If you are a girl, what do you do when you are told that you can't do something because you're a girl? Do you accept it, or do you prove them wrong?

When you learn ways to help stop violence against women, be sure to share the information with others. Sometimes your words and enthusiasm can provide more motivation than reading an article in the newspaper or listening to lectures from teachers or parents. You can also

Teens can work together in a group to develop possible solutions to the problem of violence against women in their community.

work together with officials in your school, your local or state government, or even with national or international governments to help improve the way women and girls are treated. The more people you can persuade to join in the effort to stop violence against women, the better the chances of successfully creating a safer world for women.

### ❖ QUESTIONS TO ASK YOURSELF ❖

Change needs all of us. 1) Guys: How do you talk about girls? 2) Girls: Do you let yourselves be put down? 3) Can you share the information you have learned about violence against women and the different ways to help fight it with your school or community?

# GLOSSARY

**abuser** *or* **batterer**  Person who resorts to emotional or physical abuse to gain power and control over another person.

**coalition**  A group formed to take action in support of or against social issues.

**coercion**  Use of fear or force to make someone do something he or she does not want to do.

**domestic violence** or **intimate violence** Emotional or physical abuse and attacks that take place between two people who know each other.

**feminism**  The belief that women are equal to men and deserve the same opportunities and are to be treated with the same standards as men.

**human rights**  The right of all people to be treated fairly and to live freely.

**misogyny**  Hatred of women.

**prejudice**  Opinion or judgment formed without facts or information.

**rape** Sexual intercourse through use of force or threat.

**sex offender** Person who commits and is convicted of a violent crime that involves a sexual act such as rape.

**stalk** To constantly follow someone in a threatening way.

# Organizations to Contact

The following are organizations that are working to protect the rights of women and girls in the United States and in other parts of the world. They are usually nonprofit organizations, which means that they make money from donations and contributions and can only use that money to help run the group. They need volunteers to continue their work; you can call them to volunteer or to find a chapter in your area where you can volunteer. They are also places where you or someone you know can go for help.

**Amnesty International**
322 8th Avenue, 10th Floor
New York, NY 10001
(212) 807-8400

**Do Something**
423 West 55th Street, 8th Floor
New York, NY 10019
(212) 523-1175
e-mail: do-something@aol.com

**Family Violence Prevention Fund**
383 Rhode Island Street, Suite 304
San Francisco, CA 94103
(415) 252-8900
e-mail: fund@igc.apc.org

**Human Rights Watch**
(Women's Rights Project)
485 Fifth Avenue
New York, NY 10017-6104
(212) 972-8400
e-mail: hrcnyc@hrw.org

**My Sister's Place**
P.O. Box 337
Tuckahoe, NY 10707
(914) 779-3900

**National Coalition Against Sexual Assault**
North Second Street
Harrisburg, PA 17102-3119
(717) 232-7460
e-mail: nvasc@redrose.net

**National Domestic Violence Hot Line**
(800) 799-SAFE

**Peace at Home**
95 Berkeley Street, Suite 107
Boston, MA 02116
(617) 482-9497

## Prepare Self-Defense for Women
25 East 43rd Street
New York, NY 10036
(800) 442-7273

The following groups are where men and boys can go for help if they are unable to control their emotions and turn to violence in their relationships:

| | |
|---|---|
| Amend | (303) 832-6365 |
| Common Purpose | (617) 524-7717 |
| Emerge | (617) 422-1550 |
| Raven | (314) 645-2075 |

IN CANADA

## Impact Personal Safety
(for information on Canadian self-defense programs)
(818) 757-3963

## Women Plan Toronto
736 Bathurst Street
Toronto, ON M5S 2R4
(416) 588-9751

## Ottawa Sexual Assault Support Centre Hot Line
(613) 234-2266

## Peterborough Rape Crisis Centre Hot Line
(705) 876-4444

# FOR FURTHER READING

Brownmiller, Susan. *Against Our Will: Men, Women, and Rape*. Rev. ed. New York: Bantam Books, 1988.

Chaiet, Donna. *Staying Safe on Dates*. New York: Rosen Publishing Group, 1995.

Lauder, Ronald S. *Fighting Violent Crime in America*. New York: Dodd, Mead & Co., 1985.

Levy, Barrie, ed. *Dating Violence: Young Women in Danger*. Seattle, WA: Seal Press, 1991.

Lewis, Barbara A. *The Kid's Guide to Social Action*. Minneapolis, MN: Free Spirit Publishing Inc., 1991.

Mizell, Louis, Jr. *Street Sense for Women: How to Stay Safe in a Violent World*. New York: Berkley Books, 1993.

NiCarthy, Ginny, and Davidson, Sue. *You Can Be Free: An Easy-to-Read Handbook for Abused Women*. Seattle, WA: Seal Press, 1989.

Parrot, Andrea. *Coping with Date Rape and Acquaintance Rape*. Rev. ed. New York: Rosen Publishing Group, 1995.

Russell, Diana E. H. *The Secret Trauma: Incest in*

*the Lives of Girls and Women.* New York: Basic Books, 1986.

Warshaw, Robin. *I Never Called It Rape: The Ms. Report on Recognizing, Fighting, and Surviving Date and Acquaintance Rape.* New York: Harper Perennial, 1994.

## Challenging Reading

The following are magazines you can read for more information about women, girls, and learning how you can take action in your communities.

*Ms.*
P.O. Box 57132
Boulder, CO 80322-7132.
A magazine about women around the world that talks about women's rights and feminism.

*Who Cares: A Journal of Service and Action*
1511 K Street NW, Suite 412
Washington, DC 20005
(202) 628-1691
This journal shows what young people are doing to make a difference in their communities.

# INDEX

## ABOUT THE AUTHOR

Aliza Sherman was the executive director at a domestic violence awareness group. She helped to raise media and public awareness of the problem of domestic violence. She also worked with the Mayor's Office of New York City and the Governor's Office of the State of New York. Her articles have appeared in periodicals, including *USA Today*, *Ms.*, *Executive Female*, *The Net*, and *Oracle*. She is currently working on a book about women on the Internet. She also publishes on the Internet and the World Wide Web as Cybergirl.

**PHOTO CREDITS:** Cover photo © Impact Visuals/Bill Burke; p. 2 © Impact Visuals/K. Condyles; p. 8 Impact Visuals/Steve Wewerka; pp. 10, 17 © A/P Wide World Photos; p. 23 © Image Bank/Mieke Maas; p. 25 © Image Bank; p. 31 by Maria Moreno; p. 33 © Image Bank/G & M. David de Lossy R.; p. 37 by Michael Brandt; pp. 40, 44 © Impact Visuals/Marilyn Humphries; p. 46 © Image Bank/David Brownell; p. 54 Katherine Hsu.

**PHOTO RESEARCH:** Vera Amadzadeh

**DESIGN:** Kim Sonsky